RONALD ACUNA JR.

HOW RONALD ACUNA JR. BECAME ONE OF THE BEST PLAYERS IN THE MLB

By

JACKSON CARTER

Table of Contents

LEGAL NOTES

Ronald Acuna is meant for entertainment and educational use only. All attempts have been made to present factual information in an unbiased context.

A Game Changing Talent

Baseball is more of a team sport than any other sport in existence today.

Of course, team dynamics will come into play in every type of game, but some sports focus on that more than others. For example, LeBron James can have an amazing night with his Lakers and score fifty or more points, carrying his squad across the finish line and to a major victory. Football teams are often judged by the strength of just a few positions, notably the quarterback or wide receiver. Then there are games like tennis or golf or bowling where the importance of just one player is obvious.

Athletes may say otherwise, but we know the truth. They will say that it's always a team effort and even if one player had a break-out night, a win wouldn't be possible without everyone on the unit. It's always a team effort, they say. The entire team is always important. And while there is truth in that, it's also true that most sports can live or die based on the power and strength, and hard work of one or two players at a time. There is nothing wrong with that.

But when it comes to baseball, the entire team is downright essential.

It wasn't always this way. Back in the past, the pitcher on a baseball team was usually seen as the most vital part of any team. If a team in baseball lost, the pitcher was usually blamed for giving up too many runs. If that very same team ended up winning, the same pitcher would be given accolades for seemingly striking out well and reading the opposition.

Over time, that changed. It changed because the league started allowing teams to use more than one pitcher in a game. That means that the importance and the weight of the game do not have to rest on just one pitcher anymore. Plus, training got better and batters were able to find hits more often. That means that more emphasis was put on the outfield and the infield, and the success or failure of a team was weighted more and relied upon multiple players and not just one or two players.

When you watch a modern baseball game, you see how vital everyone is. Of course, the pitcher still does run the show, but the catcher is wildly important too. Because of the catcher, an inning can be cut very short when one catches a pop fly foul ball.

Speaking of pop flies, the outfielders have shown their worth and necessity more and more over the years as they have gotten better at catching those long-range, high-in-the-sky hits. More catches mean more outs, which means a better chance at victory.

But don't forget all the basemen in the game too. They hold a very important part of the team's success in their hands. They need to be great at catching the ball, tagging the opponents, and, yes, passing the ball to other players. Again, it shows how vital each player is and how they have to work very well as a singular unit.

Yes, baseball is a team sport more than practically any other sport in the world. And this is all a long, roundabout way of saying that Ronald Acuna Jr. is a great team player.

It's been evident in the way that the outfielder has played with the Atlanta Braves since he entered the league back in 2018. It's also evident in the way he is pushing himself, getting better, and trying to do even more for the rest of his team.

But his team mentality has never been more apparent than how Acuna acted during one of the most important and successful seasons for his team. At times, he was the most vital guy on the team and was seemingly carrying the team. Later, tragedy struck and Acuna wasn't able to play with his fellow peers. Still, he remained loyal to his team and became the biggest cheerleader they had.

Acuna loves his team. He loves baseball more than anything, but he loves playing with a group of guys that he cares about and gets along with more than even that.

He has seen a lot of success—anyone playing in major league baseball has. However, Acuna has risen like a star so quickly and has become one of the most important players in the league.

But he has also had a lot of bumps in the road. And one of them was so major that it could have possibly derailed his entire career. He suffered an injury at literally the worst time of his career and missed out on something massive because of it.

Yet, that didn't stop Acuna. In fact, he came back bigger, better, and stronger than ever. And when he did return, he was ready to make up for lost time. And after some time away from the rest of the Braves, Acuna is now participating in some of the greatest baseball games the team has seen in ages, and he is a vital part of its resurgence over the last few years.

There is a lot we don't know about Acuna. Much of his early life remains shrouded in mystery. This isn't because he is trying to hide something; it's not because he is ashamed of where he came from. Instead, it shows that most of the world of baseball wasn't paying a lot of attention to Acuna before he appeared on the radar of so many in his rookie year.

Since then, Acuna has shown his potential and promise again and again and has shown that he's the sort of player that any team would be lucky and happy, and excited to have.

Acuna is a young man and it's astonishing to see someone who isn't even 25 years old become one of the most celebrated and successful players in the world of baseball. There are many young guys in the league—it's a young man's game, after all—but not most of them have tasted success like Acuna has in just a few short years. Indeed, he has already experienced the greatest honor that a baseball player in the MLB could have and he's done it all before he's even come close to 30 years old.

So, yes, we don't know a lot about his past and there is much we don't know about his future. But we do know this: Acuna is a talented superstar. He is built for baseball, he loves the game, he loves his peers, and he loves the feeling that you only get when you are working well with a team and helping them achieve victory.

Acuna isn't an old man by any means, but his story so far is long and filled with ups, downs, and many interesting facts and stories. It's an inspiring story that started far from Atlanta, Georgia but really came alive on the home field of the Atlanta Braves.

In just a few seasons, Acuna has risen through the ranks, found true superstardom, and shown the sort of man and player he really is. What's next for him? We don't know for sure, but we do know that his future would be very bright, successful, and impressive. That's just how Acuna has been since he first walked onto the field a few seasons ago.

What Makes A Baseball Star Different

There are literally hundreds of young men who play baseball in the MLB. No one would blame you if you didn't remember every single one and the stats they had and the achievements they have racked up.

The truth is that there are many players who look like, are built like, and play like Ronald Acuna Jr. At the same time, there are very few players who are as *good* as Acuna. That is because he does things that many others do, but he does them better and at a younger age. He plays like a man who has been studying baseball for generations when, in reality, he has only been doing it for a bit more than a single decade.

Some people just have natural talent and it looks like they are tailor-made and created for a certain task. For Ronald Acuna Jr., it seems like he was made to play professional baseball.

So, what do you get when you look at Acuna? What is it about him that makes him so special, so talented, and so different even though he is basically doing the same things that others do but only better?

If you want to look at things technically, Acuna is a good right-handed hitter with a wide range of hitting options. There are many players in the MLB who hit only one type of pitch or swing in only one type of way. When you have seen them bat one time, you have seen them do it thousands of times.

That's not Acuna; he is versatile. If a pitcher is throwing a four-seam fastball, Acuna can find it. If it's a curveball, he can connect. If it's a slider or something that switches it up at the last second, Acuna can still give it a good shot and can usually still hammer it. There are countless baseball players that can only really connect with a ball if it's in their very own respective sweet spot, but not Acuna. He can make a lot of magic out of any type of pitch.

This makes him dangerous to other teams because he can outsmart the pitcher. When you watch someone play baseball in the professional leagues, you see two people who are basically going at war: the pitcher and the hitter. It isn't a physical war—this isn't boxing, after all—but it's a mental one. The pitcher is trying to outsmart the batter. He is trying to switch things up, confuse them, and lure them into making a mistake. A mistake would be swinging at a ball that is out of bounds, scoring them a strike, and bringing them closer to being on the bench.

Meanwhile, the batter is trying to read a lot about the pitcher. They are trying to look at the pitches that came before and the type of pitcher this is. They are trying to think of all the options and what could come next. And they are trying to be careful. If they swing on something, they risk getting a strike. If they are able to read the pitch correctly and let a ball go out of bounds, they earn a ball and are one step closer to walking to first base or, better yet, hitting the ball and scoring a run or RBI or base hit.

Acuna is a smart player. He can read his opposition very well and he can put his physical power into creating hits out of the ball that most people would miss. When you look at him, his physical build and the way he holds himself differ from others, but he is remarkably effective. Sean Casey, a former big-league hitter, compared Acuna's hitting approach to that of Roberto Clemente because Acuna's natural core power and rotational torque, which enable him to hit without a backswing, keep the bat's knob pointed down at the plate, make contact, and retain barrel control. These are just baseball experts' ways of saying that he is positioned very well to make contact with the ball when he is in the batter's box.

And his mental game is second to none. He has played against hundreds of different pitchers throughout his career and he still hit the ball dozens upon dozens of times. His batting average, which is .278, is quite good for a young player who has only been in the MLB for a few seasons. Keep in mind that anything over .250 is typically considered quite good and the closer a player is to .300, the better. In fact, only the best of the best hit .300, and Acuna is getting closer and closer to being there.

Acuna has hit nearly 500 home runs since he joined the league back in 2018, which is a major feat for the young 25-year-old. He has been at bat over 1,700 times and has earned nearly 500 home runs, which means that when his career is all over, he may very well have a home run a third of the time.

This isn't by chance. This isn't luck. It is very important before you read about and uncover the story of Acuna that you see that he is a very smart, talented, and accomplished baseball player who really does understand the game better than most players.

He doesn't just understand his opponents and the rules of the game. In addition, he understands how he can be a better player and how even the way he holds himself, runs and moves around the field is very important to finding success on the field.

Because of that, you can see the way Acuna has fine-tuned his physicality and movements to become a better player. He didn't always start that way, but Acuna now begins off on the path of the bases with a pronounced upright stance similar to an infielder or a running back with their hands on their knees for more acceleration. Baseball expert and analyst, Harold Reynolds, who created Rickey Henderson's baserunning and fielding techniques, claims that the posture also prevents Acuna from swaying or tipping off fielders for base stealing.

He's 25 years old but he has the sort of knowledge and expertise about the game that people usually only get after studying it for many, many years. He isn't intent on just hitting the ball; he is focused on making sure that he is an all-around, well-made, solid, reliable baseball player who hits the ball but also reads his opponents and moves with total ease on the field.

Whether he is getting ready to bat or in the outfield, Acuna is going to give it his all. He is going to adapt to whoever he is playing against and he is going to be tuned in and focused, playing with 100%

determination and desire to win. He will rely on his other teammates and he will be incredibly reliable too. He knows he is part of a team and he knows that the better he is, the better the rest of the team and the better their chances of succeeding.

Again, he is more than a baseball player. He is a *team* member and that is actually a very different thing indeed.

You know what sort of player he is and hopefully, if you were to watch him on your TV tonight, you would pick up on some of the attributes listed that make him so special.

But there are other questions about Acuna. Where did he come from? What made him want to play baseball? And how long did it take him to the United States and actually become a professional baseball player in the MLB? What makes Ronald Acuna Jr. Ronald Acuna Jr.? What has happened in his life that has created such a laser-focused, determined and essential player in the modern world of baseball?

Well, like many successful athletes, Acuna first fell in love with the game at an early age. And like many successful athletes, his desire to play the sport was practically bred into him and runs through his DNA. If you were to look at where he came from and how he was raised and who raised him, you wouldn't be a bit surprised to see Ronald Acuna Jr. on the field today.

Ronald Acuna Jr is the epitome of someone who loves baseball, who has studied it for years, and has turned himself into the ultimate baseball machine, not just for him and his fame and fortune, but also for his team.

Acuna's story and his love for the game started years ago in a country far from America, but one where baseball has been thriving for decades.

Dreaming Of America's Past Time From A Distant Land

On December 18, 1997, Ronald was born in La Guaira, Venezuela. This is a part of the world where sports are beloved almost more than in America. There are many reasons for this. First, people just love to watch a group play together and take down their opponents in ways that are only possible via sports. Secondly, certain sports don't require any money to play, which means that even the most destitute people can create a team to play a sport like soccer or baseball.

And sports are a way for people to escape from poverty, provide for their families, and create a brand-new life for themselves made possible solely by the power of their skills and determination.

You have seen this again and again throughout history. There are talented players who are able to break free of the restraints of poverty by devoting their time and energy to a sport that can take them far from home. There are many people from all over the world who have become superstars in America after growing up in a country far away from the US.

Sport is a passport for many people, especially those who are eager to provide for themselves and their families. But it takes a lot of work. It takes a lot of dedication. It takes a lot of time and effort. This is something that most young athletes learn right away. It's about more than just being talented and skilled at a sport. It's about really devoting a lot of time to enhancing skills and practicing, as well as learning the ins and outs of a game. Every nook and cranny and minor feature of a sport needs to be understood and completely mastered if someone wishes to take it on as a career full-time.

No one knows that better than Acuna's father, Ronald Acuna Sr. That's because he followed a path much like his son's, just years before him and without much success. Yes, both Ronald and his father shared a love of baseball and it was this love that brought them together and also instilled the sort of drive and dedication into Ronald that he would need to make it in the big leagues.

In many ways, Ronald Acuna Jr. knew that he was going to pour himself into baseball from a young age, not just because he loved the sport so much but also because he saw what it meant to his father as well. He never made any secret of the fact that he started to really love baseball because it was something he had in common with his dad. He also has never hidden the fact that he saw that prospering in baseball was a chance for him to make his dad proud and build upon the success he had. All children want to make their parents proud and young Ronald saw excelling at baseball as a chance to do just that.

Not a whole lot is known about Ronald Acuna Jr's early family life. Sure enough, his mother Leonelis Blanco's background is mostly unknown, but there has been a lot of publicity and media attention about his father, Ronald Sr. This is because his dad played baseball in the Major League Baseball representing Venezuela at the 2011 Pan American Games.

But it wasn't just his father who played the game and instilled a love for it into his son from an early age. Ronald's grandpa, uncle, and several relatives were all professional baseball players, adding to the athletic background of his family. This means that from the very beginning of his life, Ronald knew a lot about baseball and saw it all around him. He saw how the crowd reacted to a great game, he saw the sort of fame and accolades that could come to someone who mastered the game and became a successful professional player.

Acuna also saw that playing the game well could help someone provide for and take care of their family and friends. When Ronald Acuna Jr. was growing up, his home country was experiencing a lot of financial problems and poverty was seeping into almost everyone's life. The entire country was facing a lot of problems. And while Ronald's father had found some success playing sports, Acuna really did want to step up and provide for his family.

He saw baseball as a way to do that. And the country he came from had a long history of people really diving head first into the sport and finding great fame, fortune, and success in it.

Baseball in Venezuela

Baseball has been a huge part of Venezuela for more than a generation now. Many people think of baseball as an American sport. And of course, it definitely did start in the United States and remains a staple of America's persona and the idea that many people have of the country. Indeed, baseball is often said to be as American as "apple pie" or the flag.

But it has been thriving down in Venezuela for decades now and, in many ways, it has literally transformed the country and the young people living in it. There are so many people who enjoy great success and financial benefits by playing baseball and they have been able to travel the world, become celebrities, live their dreams, and help out their family and friends. Because of that, baseball has been seen as something very special to the people of Venezuela ever since it arrived there more than 100 years ago.

Yet, how did this American creation come to find itself exploding and becoming a major part of the culture down in South America? It started in the early days of baseball, long before the MLB had a cultural grip on the globe. Venezuelan students who had attended American institutions brought baseball to the nation. At that time, baseball was still nothing compared to what it is now, but it was definitely booming in the US.

The traveling Venezuelan students saw just how great the game was and how it was bringing in crowds of hundreds, if not thousands. They also saw how great the game was for the crowds and how excited they were. And they also saw how simple the game was.

Baseball has never been like football, with so many specific rules and difficult procedures that make it hard to play unless you have a lot of proper playing and ample space. With baseball, that wasn't needed. In reality, all that was needed to play baseball was a field big enough for four bases, a ball, a stick to hit it with, and players that wanted to partake.

The rules of baseball are very easy to follow and that is one of the reasons why it has spread all over the world with ease. It doesn't take a rocket scientist to figure out baseball. Nowadays, there are so many statistics and little intricate factoids and things to keep in mind. But back in the late 1800s, that wasn't the case. Back then, baseball was far simpler. You stood on home base, you swung at the ball, and you attempted to get around all three bases and make it back home.

You will see that the sports that have found the most success all over the world are the ones that are easy to understand and don't require any sort of translation of cultures. Baseball, soccer, and other sports can be played anywhere on the planet because you can easily pick up the rules and figure out how to play. That is definitely the case with baseball; it stood the chance to really thrive in Venezuela or any other country and it didn't need a lengthy explanation.

The students traveling to the States saw this and they imagined that the kids and friends they knew back home in South America would absolutely love baseball. They also loved playing the game themselves and they wanted to spread the joy and excitement that came with the game back home. So, they brought the game back home and spread the word about it. They immediately began to make baseball the central part of their lives and tried to find many converts who would also fall in love with the game like they did. The students taught the game to their pals in Caracas when they returned home after completing their coursework in the early 1890s.

The game of baseball soon became something that was played by many kids in the area. As predicted, students in the region really took to the game quickly and soon there was a baseball game being played every day after school was over. It didn't matter how much money or how much education the kids had. They were all equals on the baseball field and soon little baseball diamonds were popping up all over the area.

The very first organized baseball team was founded by the Franklin brothers, Augusto, Emilio, Amenodoro, and Gustavo in May 1895 under the name Caracas BBC. They were looking to take the game to the next level. They wanted it to become more than just a hobby. They wanted it to become something that could change lives, start careers, and really capture the imagination of the entire nation. So, for three months before that, the squad started training every single Sunday afternoon at a piece of undeveloped ground right next to the Quebrada Honda railway station. What started as a modest field that didn't really catch the eye of fellow countrymen was soon something that felt lush and vibrant and inviting to both players and fans. The Caracas Baseball Club Exercise Field would shortly take the name of the field.

To promote baseball, the club arranged the first official match in Venezuela. They published an advertisement for the game in May 1895, in the popular and well-respected newspaper, El Tiempo, describing it as a "new kind of Chess game, Base Bale." Two teams made up of Caracas BBC members hit the field the next day. The squads were called red and blue, with Amenodoro Franklin's blue squad prevailing by a score of 28 to 19. The Franklin brothers, Adolfo Inchausti, Alfredo Mosquera, brothers Jaime and Roberto Todd, Mariano Becerra, who were all once American students and are regarded as the game's forefathers in Venezuela, as well as three Cubans who lived in Caracas, Manuel and Joaquin Gonzalez and Emilio Gramer, were among the participants.

Baseball was finding the success that many people expected, but it was finding it far faster than expected and was soon getting a lot of attention in the media and newspapers of the region. For example, the first official game was covered by the newspaper, El Tiempo, but that actually did not help because many viewers thought they were going to see a chess match due to poor wording in the newspaper. The newspaper writers were trying to describe baseball to people who had never seen the game before, so they compared it to chess, a game that everyone knows. But this led to a lot of confusion because people in Venezuela thought they were going to watch a *literal* chess match, not a game that was *like* one.

The game's recap the next day focused more on the setting than on the actual play: "With no disguises, flowers, candies, or other reddish items, it appeared to be a carnival on a Sunday. Everyone was so happy that that afternoon not even one complaint about the

Republic's poverty could be heard. People enjoyed themselves, at least the portion of the population with more resources to do so, as in previous eras."

Another newspaper, El Pregonero, claimed that baseball gave a lot of health as well as physical strength to the human body and also happiness to anyone playing it. And with that, the game was now spreading to every corner of the country, thanks to the media. People were soon talking about this new field game that could be played just about anywhere and was creating a huge fanbase in the United States.

The first baseball images to be published in the country appeared in the journal, El Cojo Ilustrado, three months later, raising awareness around the country and attracting more fans and people who were curious to learn the ins and out of the game. A few days after the game, the proprietor of Caracas Beer Company built Stand del Este, the nation's first baseball stadium, with seats and construction dimensions modeled after American rules. It was created close to Petare train station in a Caracas suburb. It was obvious that the entire city had become enthralled with the new sport.

With an official stadium now residing in the country, people all over Venezuela were falling madly in love with baseball and soon diamonds were being constructed in empty fields, behind schools, and in every nook and cranny of the country. It had only been a few years, but it was quickly rivaling soccer as the most popular pastime for the rest of the country.

By the turn of the century, the game was hugely well-liked. William H. Phelps founded a baseball business in Maracaibo in 1912, and he subsequently organized a league with three teams called "The Red", "The Blue", and "The Black" in the city. In 1920, Maracaibo had thirty clubs and ten ballparks, and nearby places like Valencia and Maracay also had clubs. The game swiftly spread across the city. The oldest continuously operating club in the country was established in 1917 and is today known as Navegantes del Magallanes.

Over the next few decades, some young men found great success playing the game in Venezuela and then moved to the United States to find even more success. You have to remember that back then, not many non-white players were participating in professional sports. They had separate leagues for people of color and separate leagues for white professionals.

Indeed, it was much, much harder to break through to the American crowds back then, but that would change over the years as civil rights grew and the mentality of Americans also changed and they began to accept people of color. By the time Ronald Acuna Jr. was born, there were countless foreign-born athletes who became superstars in the United States.

FINDING BASEBALL

Being born in Venezuela at the time of Acuna's birth was to come into a culture that really loved, lived, and breathed baseball. It was everywhere. So, even if his father had nothing to do with the sport, Acuna probably would have been interested in it.

But Ronald's family, aside from his father, really loved baseball and so it was even easier for him to fall madly in love with the sport from a very young age. The oldest of Ronald's four siblings, Luisangel, found a lot of great success on the baseball diamond from before the time Ronald was born. Today, he is now a member of the Texas Rangers. In total, Ronald has four siblings, although not a whole lot is known about them. But we do know that his family life was good early on; he spent long days in school and then long nights outside in the humid Venezuelan heat learning how to play baseball and spending time with his brothers and sisters. He was becoming a baseball fanatic before he could even speak.

Not much is known about Ronald Acuna Jr. when he was a youth, but he definitely did study hard in these early years. He also studied the game of baseball, taught to him by his older siblings and definitely by his father, who was trying to impart knowledge of the game to his young son. Although Ronald Acuna Sr.

had found some success and even some fame playing baseball, he expected—and wanted—better things for his children.

He saw a lot of great potential in Ronald and he wanted to nurture his skills and help him become even better, with the hopes that maybe someday he could support himself by playing the game he loved. But Ronald Sr. knew two things about this concept: he could only do it if Ronald Jr. had skills and he would only agree to it if his son really and truly wanted to play baseball professionally. While his kid definitely did enjoy the game, Ronald Sr. never wanted to force this lifestyle on him and was always sure to let him know that he had many options for his life. He could be anything he wanted to and he didn't *have* to devote his life to the game unless he wanted to.

It quickly became clear that Ronald Jr. really did want to play baseball full-time. It was not a fad; it was not a phase he was working his way through. He really did want to devote all of his time and energy to the game. He would watch old games that his father played and he would study the game nightly. There were very few days that Ronald Jr. wasn't out on the baseball field hitting balls and trying to perfect his catching abilities.

Ronald Sr. saw great things in his young son. He had the sort of drive that would make him a better player. This drive would mean he would never give up, he would never stop trying, and he would never stop demanding more from himself. But there was more to Ronald Jr.'s power and promise. He was naturally talented. He was a smart kid and he was able to read his opponents incredibly well, even from a young age. Ronald Sr. knew just how important this would be moving forward. He knew that if Ronald Jr. was the type of player who could understand and comprehend, and get a good reading on pitchers and other players, he would be leagues ahead of other young men trying to enter the league.

He was still a little rough around the edges; he needed to evolve his abilities and really dive headfirst into the game and truly treat it like a full-time job. But if he was willing to treat baseball as his one and only passion and his future, Ronald Sr. was willing and ready, and eager to help him become the sort of baseball player he wanted.

THE PATH TO THE MLB

Ronald Acuna Sr. and his son didn't expect college in his future. This was for multiple reasons: namely, college was very expensive and hard to get into. Secondly, it would take away more time from Ronald attempting to make his way into the MLB in America and finding international success in the game.

So instead of planning to push his way through high school and college, Ronald Jr. instead plotted a path that would get him through his studies in high school while also becoming a better baseball player. By the time he graduated, he would be prepared and ready to make his move to the MLB and take his chance at finding fame and fortune in the states.

By the time both Ronald and his dad decided upon this plan, they didn't have a whole lot of time to enact it. That meant that they'd have to work overtime and spend a lot of time perfecting his game, pushing himself, and propelling his skills to the next level.

So, his days were spent like this: waking up early in the morning, going to school, coming home after school, and playing baseball and studying the game until the sun went down. Day in and day out, this was the life of young Ronald Acuna Jr.

In just a few short years, Acuna had really improved the type of player he was. The way he held the bat, the way he was versatile and swung at nearly any type of pitch, the way he ran around the bases and the way he had a sixth sense about his opponents were all learned in his early-to-mid teenage years.

COMING TO AMERICA

By the time he was approaching the part of the plan that required him to take a stab at being in the MLB, both Acuna and his dad felt he was truly ready. But they had to do more than impress the people in Venezuela. They also had to impress American MLB scouts for him to find the sort of success his talent was capable and worthy of.

Performing for baseball scouts is a fine art that not many people are ready to master. If young players do well at it, they can become professional athletes in a short period of time and can soon skyrocket to the level of players like Juan Soto, Freddie Freeman, and others.

But if someone whiffs it and doesn't perform well for scouts, their chances of ever making it in the MLB or any professional league are greatly reduced.

What is a scout? Basically, they are people who work on behalf of teams in the league. Their job…their sole responsibility is to judge and monitor up-and-coming talent and decide who is ready for the next step. Who should teams take a chance on? Who is ready to be brought to the minor leagues or the developmental league and who is ready to just move straight to the big game and play major league baseball? This is all determined by a baseball scout and, as you can see, a lot is riding on how well young athletes do in front of them.

A baseball scout will judge a player based on many things, not just their ability to hit the ball. You have to remember that a professional baseball team is like a puzzle, and it is always looking for certain pieces that are necessary for the time being. Maybe they need a pitcher, but maybe they need a pitcher who can also hit the ball into left field. Maybe they need outfielders, but maybe they need outfielders who can also be catchers or can steal bases. A baseball team is constantly trying to tweak itself, perfect itself, and fill any voids with as few players as possible.

In 2014, the Atlanta Braves happened to be looking for someone exactly like Ronald Acuna Jr. They wanted youth, they wanted power and skill at the plate, they wanted versatility, and they also wanted someone with smarts who was able to play on any part of the field, but most specifically the outfield. Well, it just so happened that Ronald was a pro at playing outfield and that was very, very appealing to the scouts monitoring him for the Braves.

Because of this, he looked like the whole package and Atlanta moved fast to sign him to a deal, but it wasn't the type of deal he wanted and originally envisioned.

In July 2014, Acuna agreed to a deal for $100,000 as an unrestricted foreign free agent with the Atlanta Braves. This meant that he was on retainer and could be called upon by the Braves in Atlanta if they wanted or by any of their associated minor league teams. Sure enough, just a year later, Acuna had his debut with the Gulf Coast Braves before being moved up to the Danville Braves later that year. He batted in 55 games for both clubs. He made 4 runs, 18 RBIs, and 16 bases stolen in 269 at-bats.

That was a great start for Acuna in America. He was finally playing the game he loved in the country he had wished to move to since he was a youth. He was showing coaches, players, and fans that he was an up-and-coming talent to keep an eye on. And sure enough, there was soon talk of him possibly playing in the major league in no distant time.

Few people thought or expected Acuna to remain in the minor leagues. Many people expected him to achieve more greatness and find his way into the big leagues very soon.

His time in the minor league had a setback that sadly foreshadowed the misfortune that would come within a few years. Because of an injury, Acuna only played for the Gulf Coast Braves as well as the Rome Braves for 42 games combined in 2016. Although he didn't get to participate in as many games as he wanted, he still had a very impressive track record during those games, hitting .312/.393/.429 with four home runs and 19 RBIs.

He was attracting the attention of many baseball players and teams, but not just those in America. In fact, he was invited to and participated in the Australian Baseball League for the Melbourne Aces in 2016 and was selected as an ABL All-Star. This was a great honor and one that Acuna didn't really see coming. His plan was to always impress in the minor leagues and then segue seamlessly into the major leagues. But a short trip to Australia allowed him to raise his profile even more and perfect his skills in the hopes of becoming a major league star soon.

He was bouncing all over the globe and all over the minor leagues, and this was leading to more and more compliments, attention, and offers. Acuna was told he could join the Arizona Fall League and he agreed to it. After accepting the offer, Acuna was assigned to the Peoria Javelinas following the conclusion of the 2017 minor league regular season. He didn't play with them for many games, but he certainly had a huge impact on the team during his time with them.

Acuna played in 23 games for the AFL, slashing .325/.414/.639 with seven home runs while also winning the league title and earning MVP honors, becoming the league's youngest MVP.

He was an MVP at a young age and he had played for multiple teams in many parts of the country and even on many continents. This was obviously a successful career already, but Acuna wanted more. His end goal was to always play in the major leagues. He had a deal with the Atlanta Braves but had yet to officially play a game with that team. But that's what he wanted and that's what he was playing and fighting for.

He envisioned a career where he would become a starting outfielder for the Braves. There was some frustration at that point that it hadn't become reality yet, but Acuna knew he had to just keep his head down, continue playing hard, and prove himself to every single team that offered him a deal. He didn't care if he was playing in Australia or Antarctica;

Acuna was going to pour himself into the game and show that he really had what it took to enter the next phase of his career.

He didn't want to wait anymore, but he wasn't going to give up any time soon.

Thankfully, he didn't have to wait much longer.

THE BIG SHOW

He had only been playing professional baseball for a few years now, but Acuna was on the verge of finally achieving the goals he had always wanted. He could feel it. The more and more he played, the more he saw himself becoming better and more skilled and important for the squads he played with. It wasn't just the fact that he had been awarded MVP for the AFL; he was also feeling how teams were relying on him, turning to him, and needing him to find success.

And he was getting a lot more attention in the press too. There were many newspapers, websites, and analysts keeping a close eye on Acuna even after just a few seasons. They saw that he could be a breakout start in the MLB in the nearest future and most people thought he was very, very close to officially starting for a major league team.

Acuna entered the 2018 season as the top possibility in Major League Baseball according to Baseball America. Not only that, but he was also ranked in second place by MLB.com after Japanese superstar-in-the-making, Shohei Ohtani, which showed that now millions of people were looking at Acuna as possibly the next big thing.

He wanted to strike while the iron was hot and he wanted to really make an impact and take the next step in his career. He was still toiling away in the minor leagues, even after spending time at spring training and knocking the socks off of many fans. He was ready to become the next big thing that people thought he could be. He just needed his team to sign off on him and let him have the chance to prove himself on the biggest stage possible.

FINALLY A BRAVE

It had only been a few short years, but it felt like a lifetime to Ronald Acuna Jr. He was desperate to reach his full potential and play in the major leagues and really make himself into the baseball superstar he knew he could be. He had proven himself in the minor leagues, and all over the world, and he was eager to finally make that impact on the big field in Atlanta.

His time finally came. The Braves then promoted Acuna to the major leagues on April 25, 2018. His major promotion created headlines all over the web and got Braves fans very excited. Acuna was now the youngest athlete in the MLB, but everyone who had been paying attention to his career so far knew what they were getting with the young star: he was fast, he was smart, he was very versatile and capable of doing just about anything in the batter's box and the outfield.

He wasn't just ready to play in the major league; he was downright desperate to do so. He knew there was a lot of pressure on him now that he was going to officially play for the Braves, but he had shown again and again that he could handle pressure and the expectations that die-hard fans and teams had for him.

In his opening game, Kevin Shackelford gave Acuna his first professional hit in a game against the Cincinnati Reds. He went 1 for 5 for the game as a whole, scoring the go-ahead run in the second-to-last inning as the Braves prevailed 5-4. It was a good, if not amazing, start, but Acuna felt so excited and yet so comfortable and in his skin playing on such a big level. He felt like this was something he had been working for, for years. He had spent nearly all his life expecting and anticipating this moment and he knew that he was going to deliver on his promises.

His next game ended up being a very good one. Acuna blasted his very first MLB home run against the Reds the next day off Homer Bailey. He went 3 for 4 for the game, which the Braves won 7-4. This red-hot start to his career was drawing a lot of attention and there was talk of him becoming a starter for the team and perhaps the most reliable outfielder on the squad.

Sadly, yet another injury-plagued young Acuna and it sent him off the field and onto the injury list. For the next few weeks, Acuna watched the games from the sidelines, attempting to rehab from his injury and get back into playing shape, ready to help his team again and build upon the great start he already had. He spent a bit more time in the minor league during his injury period and was once again ready to join the Braves when the All-Star Game rolled around.

THE BIG RETURN

After the All-Star break, Acuna frequently hit leadoff in the lineup. It was obvious that Acuna had spent his time away from the team focused on how he could be a better player. He came back with a brand-new bag of tricks and new tools he could use to become a better player.

For instance, this is when Acuna changed the way he stood and held himself as he batted. This was because he spoke with Kevin Seitzer and listened to the sound advice he gave him. Right away, this seemingly minor change had a noticeable positive impact on his performance.

He was now making up for lost time and was performing even better than he had in the opening of his major league career. On August 13, 2018, Acuna made MLB history by being the fourth player to smash a home run to start consecutive games of a doubleheader when taking on the Miami Marlins. In an amazing feat that is rarely replicated, Acuna had also hit a home run in each of his previous four games, making him the youngest player to do it since the year 1920, nearly 100 years before.

Acuna was now off to the races and started to break records and really prove himself as one of the most valuable players on one of the best teams in the entire MLB. Ronald became just the sixth batter in Braves history and the youngest player in big league history to smash home runs in five straight games after hitting one off Trevor Richards on August 14. It's incredibly hard to hit *one* home run and the idea of hitting another home run motivated Acuna to get his next home run right away against Adam Conley in the very same game, becoming the first player to ever hit two home runs in a single game.

On August 23, when Acuna faced the Marlins again, he smashed another home run and was then hit by another pitch. He received the MLB Rookie of the Month Award for August as a result of his performance. On September 2, Acuna smashed his seventh home run, tying Marquis Grissom's franchise record for such home runs in a season for the Braves. Acuna then broke the franchise record for leadoff home runs in a matchup versus the Boston Red Sox just three days later.

On September 9, Acuna's stellar season continued as he hit his 25th home run, becoming the fifth player in the history of Major League Baseball to do so while still under the age of 21. Then on September 22, Acuna stole his fifteenth base to join Alex Rodriguez and Mike Trout as some of the only players in MLB history to have a 25-15 season while still under the age of twenty. Acuna played a total of 111 MLB games with the 2018 Braves, batting.293 with 26 home runs and 64 RBIs.

After an incredible regular season and a very strong showing in the postseason, Acuna was now primed to accept a huge honor that only the best of the best had experienced in the past.

Throughout the season, there was talk that Ronald was on track to become the Rookie of the Year for the National League. Indeed, his name was mentioned again and again as the best newcomer in his league, let alone the entire MLB. And his number of home runs and terrific outfield work only made him more attractive to those voting on the coveted trophy.

It wasn't very often that a player had a rookie season like Ronald Acuna Jr. was having. Therefore, when he received the National League Rookie of the Year award on November 12, many people and all his fans were elated…but not that surprised. It just made sense. He had earned the honor; he had earned the trophy. It was plain to see and it was an award that felt tailor-made for this young man who had come bursting into the major leagues.

After the season he had, the award he received, and the promise he showed, the Braves wanted to be in the Acuna business in a big, big way. They wanted more of Ronald—a lot more. Because of that, Acuna and the Braves reached an agreement on an eight-year, $100 million contract on April 2, 2019. It was a monster deal and one that showed just how much he was valued. It wasn't often that players were signed to deals that were that huge and that long-lasting, but the Braves didn't want to risk losing this young star and envisioned a future in which he was a central part of the team literally for years to come.

For the future 2027 and 2028 seasons, the contract had team choices, which gave the Braves a bit more power and choice at that point. Once again, Ronald made history. This time, Acuna made baseball history by signing the sport's first deal for at least $100 million at the age of 21. As you can see, this just wasn't something that happened often in the league and it showed how valuable and important Acuna was. He was shaping up to be a generational talent who could be a huge part of the league for many years to come.

Perhaps, one of the most stunning things about Acuna's major deal was that it was the biggest ever for a player with less than a full season in a major league. And the contract wasn't the only indicator to show how much attention, fame, and respect he was garnering: he also received an invitation to participate in the 2019 Major League Baseball Home Run Derby and was selected as the National League's starting outfielder for the 2019 All-Star Game at midseason.

Acuna faced Marlins pitcher, Tayron Guerrero, on August 9 and hit his thirty-first home run of the year. But he didn't slow down after that and kept adding on the HRs as the season wore on. On September 19, Acuna hit his forty-first home run, but that amazing news was dampened by another injury that reared its ugly little head. In the Braves' last series of the current season, Acuna disclosed a slight injury and rested for the remainder of the season.

All in all, it was a remarkable opening season that would be spoken about for years to come. It is true that it didn't end in the best way imaginable, but it was still a stunning rookie year for the young phenom. In the end, Ronald hit .280/.365/.518/.883 during that first season, leading the National League in runs, home runs, and stolen bases with 127.

Dealing With The Pandemic

Acuna was ready to keep up the amazing progress and pace he set in his first year in the MLB, but his season—and everyone's life—would be radically transformed the following season due to the coronavirus pandemic. Sadly, it was the start of a string of bad luck that would change his career, sideline him repeatedly, but also show his worth to the team.

When COVID came around, baseball was thrown into disarray. Games were canceled, players were sick, and something as simple as traveling across the country to play a game was literally impossible and ultimately life-threatening. Eventually, the MLB was able to make some changes, figure out a plan, and forge ahead in a brand-new world that was altered by the pandemic.

Despite all the changes and the confusion and the anxiety and oddness of the post-COVID baseball world, the Braves set a league record by winning a league-high 20th division title during that season and they also won their division yet again for the third consecutive year. And Ronald was at it once again with his stellar performances: he blasted the longest MLB home run of the year and the biggest home run ever hit at Truist Park against the Red Sox at the conclusion of the season.

In 2020, he topped the league in at bats per home run with a batting line of .250/.406/.581 with 14 home runs and 29 RBIs in 160 at-bats. He received his second Silver Slugger Award in a row and came in at number twelve in the vote for the Most Valuable Player Award.

Acuna was awarded the National League Player of the Month in April of 2021 after batting an incredible .341/.443/.705 in 24 games while hitting eight home runs, stealing three bases, driving in 18 runs, and scoring 25 runs. Acuna's walk-off home run against the New York Mets on May 19 gave the Braves a 5-4 victory.

The world had changed, the league had been thrown for a loop, but Ronald Acuna Jr. was just as powerful, impressive, and essential as he had been since the very beginning of his time with the Braves.

Sadly, all of this would be put to the most extreme test yet in the months ahead. It was going to be both a wildly successful and painfully disappointing time for the team.

THE INJURY

Acuna had quickly become one of the best, brightest, and most important parts of the team. He was a legitimate superstar, worthy of the awards he had won, and was now a fan favorite and someone who was constantly on SportsCenter, in newspapers, and was regarded as perhaps the best young player in the whole MLB.

Because of his hard work, Acuna was helping his team surge through the National League and it was becoming obvious that the team was well on its way to the World Series if they kept performing as well as they had been. As long as the team continued to perform with skill, talent, and drive, they could be hoisting the biggest trophy in the league above their heads at the end of summer.

But then something happened that would both shatter the team and also bring it closer together. And it would allow Acuna a chance to show that he's a team player in more ways than one.

Ronald had experienced multiple injuries before and they were all painful to experience, but he was about to encounter the worst one yet; one that could pull him out of rotation for the longest period of time and could force him to miss a piece of history.

Acuna was injured while attempting to field a fly ball on July 10, 2021. Right away, it was obvious that the injury was bad—really bad. It was the worst thing that had happened to Ronald since he entered the league. It was so bad, in fact, that Acuna was carried off the pitch on a stretcher.

He had been doing so well in the weeks before and was truly the breakout star of his team, but now a new reality was facing them and altering their plans in some drastic, scary ways. Acuna's 2021 season was abruptly halted after an MRI revealed just how extensive the injury was.

That was it. No more baseball for Ronald Acuna Jr. This was awful news not only for the player but also for his team. That is because he had become such a vital part of the squad and its spirit and attitude as well as its entire culture. But with the injury he suffered, moving forward was simply impossible.

Acuna hit .283/.394/.596 in 82 games in 2021, with 24 home runs, 52 RBIs, and 17 stolen bases. At the time of his injury, he was the major league leader in runs scored with 72. This raised a lot of questions: was there any chance of him recovering and coming back by the time the World Series came around? More importantly, would the team even need him in the World Series? Would they even get to the World Series without Acuna on the field?

This was not the outcome that Acuna wanted nor was it the one he had in mind, but he was going to make the most of it. He was still a member of the team, he was still a very important part of his squad, and he was proud to sit in the dugout for the remainder of the season, rooting them on and giving his input and being the biggest cheerleader possible.

Of course, it was painful for him to see his team continue to play games without him. It was also painful when he saw them make the World Series and he was not allowed to step on the field because he had not healed yet. But even though Ronald would admit that it was hard to see all this and not participate, he was still enthusiastic, happy, connected to his team, and a major part of their historic World Series run.

Even without Acuna on the field, the Braves managed to win the 2021 World Series. And who was in the dugout in the final moments, pumping his fists in the air and cheering on his squad? It was none other than Ronald Acuna Jr., their star player and now the biggest supporter around.

The Braves were the biggest team in the MLB now and although he was injured, Acuna was one of its biggest stars. Yes, he was still recovering when the next season began, but there was an end in sight to his rehab and the time for his return was quickly approaching.

And when he was taken off the injury list in April, people were beyond ready to see him suit up and play again. The Braves' most exciting young player was back. He was gone for so long—too long—but Ronald Acuna Jr. was once again ready to make up for lost time.

MORE FROM JACKSON CARTER BIOGRAPHIES

My goal is to spark the love of reading in young adults around the world. Too often children grow up thinking they hate reading because they are forced to read material they don't care about. To counter this we offer accessible, easy to read biographies about sportspeople that will give young adults the chance to fall in love with reading.

Go to the Website Below to Join Our Community

https://mailchi.mp/7cced1339ff6/jcbcommunity

Or Find Us on Facebook at

www.facebook.com/JacksonCarterBiographies

As a Member of Our Community You Will Receive:

First Notice of Newly Published Titles

Exclusive Discounts and Offers

Influence on the Next Book Topics

Don't miss out, join today and help spread the love of reading around the world!

OTHER WORKS BY JACKSON CARTER BIOGRAPHIES

Patrick Mahomes: The Amazing Story of How Patrick Mahomes Became the MVP of the NFL

Donovan Mitchell: How Donovan Mitchell Became a Star for the Salt Lake City Jazz

Luka Doncic: The Complete Story of How Luka Doncic Became the NBA's Newest Star

The Eagle: Khabib Nurmagomedov: How Khabib Became the Top MMA Fighter and Dominated the UFC

Lamar Jackson: The Inspirational Story of How One Quarterback Redefined the Position and Became the Most Explosive Player in the NFL

Jimmy Garoppolo: The Amazing Story of How One Quarterback Climbed the Ranks to Be One of the Top Quarterbacks in the NFL

Zion Williamson: The Inspirational Story of How Zion Williamson Became the NBA's First Draft Pick

Kyler Murray: The Inspirational Story of How Kyler Murray Became the NFL's First Draft Pick

Do Your Job: The Leadership Principles that Bill Belichick and the New England Patriots Have Used to Become the Best Dynasty in the NFL

Turn Your Gaming Into a Career Through Twitch and Other Streaming Sites: How to Start, Develop and Sustain an Online Streaming Business that Makes Money

From Beginner to Pro: How to Become a Notary Public